True Love

Love Secrets Before
and
After Marriage

Brenda Lowery

There is love that lasts for a summer, a year, or a lifetime. In fact, it does not matter how long your relationships last if they bring you some experience and happiness. In this case, you are going to keep the memories about them like something really precious.

Philosophers, mystics, and esotery scientists have always been trying to explain the mystery of love. Let us get to know the most popular theories. It is up to you to choose the one, which looks the most reliable.

Table of Contents

The Theories

The first theory is based on the analysis of biochemical processes that are going on in a person's body when he or she is in love.

In science terms, love is a biochemical process, which is going on in a human body. So, let us try to understand what one of the most fundamental feelings on the planet actually is.

Love starts with infatuation. Infatuation is a kind of sign for the body. It means that a long-desired person is somewhere near by. In itself, infatuation is a sudden, uncontrollable, and strong feeling but it does not last long.

Do not confuse infatuation with flirting! Infatuation triggers general changes in the body:

— The heart starts beating fast (it seems like it is trying to get out);

— The palms are sweating, the person can feel cold and hot periodically;

— Shivering rather often;

— The pupils get dilated, but the light is not the reason;

— The feeling of flight; he or she believes that nothing is impossible;

— The perception of everything around increases;

— Never hungry; he or she does not want to eat anything;

— Attention gets distracted, it is practically impossible to concentrate on something;

— Love for everybody around, never angry;

— Some hidden talents can be revealed, for example, for poetry or painting;

— Desires to act absurdly.

These signs are provoked by serious hormonal fluxes. That is why love is considered to be a kind of obfuscation.

Love emotions produce a release of *dopamine*. It becomes the reason for euphoria, unprecedented energy, and inspiration. Too much of dopamine makes us act foolishly or heroically. We forget about danger and social conventions.

However, the wild mood swing and abnormal behavior are provoked not only by *dopamine*, but also by *serotonin*. Serotonin is one of biogenic amines. The more serotonin we have in the brain, the happier we are. Lack of serotonin, in its turn, leads to depressions. Our moods and feelings depend only on the biochemistry of the brain. In other words, excessive sociability and talkativeness, love for all the world and thinking that the world is perfect – all these things are the signs and the result of a good serotonin dose.

People in love are often sleepless. This fact is related to other hormones. Excessive energy, excitement, worrying, fast heart-beating, and leg weakness – it is all about adrenaline and noradrenaline. These are the hormones, which make us spend sleepless nights, thinking about a person we love.

While we are thinking about a significant other, the body starts producing hormones automatically, just like it is producing saliva while we are thinking about a lemon. It is not necessary to see a lemon; it is enough to imagine it. Thus, when we imagine a person we love before falling asleep, we actually get too much adrenaline that keeps us awake.

A person in love feels and thinks not like all the rest. The central nervous system produces *enkephalines* (morphine-like peptides, which are involved in anesthesia, decrease the functioning of the gastrointestinal tract, etc). Alongside with enkephalines, there is also a well-known hormone of happiness – endorphin. The elevated level of endorphin provokes positive emotions. Enkephalines and endorphins work just like drugs. They make us feel good, but it does not last long. That is why infatuation dies very quickly.

Infatuation increases the level of neuropeptides; they make us feel calm and safe when we are close to a beloved one. In other words, when we are next to a significant other, our brains react in such a way that it works like a tranquilizing drug.

Our emotions are nothing more but a reflection of our inner worlds. This reflection is possible due to certain receptors. The substances contained in a natural smell of every human being – pheromones – affect these receptors. Thus, pheromones trigger biochemical changes in the brain.

However, it is not only about hormonal fluxes and natural smells.

Appearance (body), swagger, voice, and eyes play a very important role. All these things can make the closest and dearest person out of a stranger. That is why lovers feel like they have known each other for ages, though they met quite recently. They are willing to be together till the end of their lives. Infatuation makes people treat a partner's actions and words one-sidedly. They are likely to chant praises to him or her without noticing obvious drawbacks.

We love the one who can give us healthy and bright children. When a woman meets a man, she pays attention to his appearance. Is he fit enough to have good sex? Are his shoulders broad? Does he have a nice butt? At the same time she is reflexively trying to decode his natural smell. What about his immunity and sex hormones level? Are we compatible from the genetic point? His DNA should be different from hers as much as possible to prevent the birth of a child with a genetically determined disease. If she does not like his smell, no love can start. It is not a father of her children. What about his intelligence and spirituality? These are the last things to estimate in case everything mentioned above is OK.

Infatuation

When a woman sees an attractive man her body says, "I need him, I can have good children by him!" She feels sexual drive and excitement, "How can I get him?" The stress hormone (noradrenaline) gets into the blood. The perception of everything around is increasing, the heart is beating fast, and the eyes are shining. It is hard to sleep during the night; she is worrying during the day. She seldom feels hungry and loses her weight. Bingo! They are together at last and have sex. Stress and adrenaline are decreasing. *Neurohormones* of ecstasy, joy, and pleasure – *dopamine* and *serotonin* – are increasing instead. Dopamine is a hormone of purpose and focusing on a single idea, it enhances passion and energy.

Those who have a lot of dopamine cannot notice anything around except a beloved one; they are able to do everything for him or her. The mood is deviating all the time, "It seems he loves me, I feel like flying", or "It seems he does not love me, I'd better go and hang myself"...

In the end, (in the most typical cases) infatuation leads to the dominance of serotonin. This hormone provides a stable joyful mood, "I'm great, and my partner is also great". It is a right time to dive into poetry or do something really difficult. Thanks to the increase of dopamine and serotonin, people can experience romance they are dreaming about. To tell the truth, identical biochemical shifts are typical of people who play roulette, smoke weed, or suffer from schizophrenia... Forget it! Romantic hormones are working hard for a year to make lovers have sex as often as possible for the pregnancy. Then their level goes down. Some people look at each other soberly and drift apart.

Actually, infatuation is a little like a nervous breakdown that is uncontrollable. It is quite natural because it is all about chemical processes, which affect the brain.

Infatuation is a bright, deep, and cool feeling. It can be compared only to the desire to live when a person is under a sentence of death. As a rule, it is only an illusion. It is only a dream, a hope for happiness, which lovers build in their minds. Thus, all these positive emotions are triggered not by a partner, but by his or her image in mind.

Carl Jung's theory suggests that infatuation is a product of our unconscious minds. Unconsciousness is a number of psychological tools, which a person is not actually aware of. These tools presuppose everything that a person builds in his mind during the lifetime.

Unconsciousness is characterized by the two main stages of a person's development in the past and in the future. The basic unconscious processes include the material from the past, or rather the material given to him or her by the evolution. The processes of a higher level (the second stage) are about the potentials of a person's mind, which can come true only if the person keeps developing spiritually.

But until these potentials haven't come true to the full extent, they come into his or her life unexpectedly and fragmentary. It happens in the form of the greatest feelings. A person tries to bring these feelings into the present day, to master and rule them. But the principle, which generates such emotions, is unknown, and we all are subconsciously trying to link them with another person who happened to be nearby at the moment when the greatest feelings arose. That is a start of infatuation. We just link the best moments of our lives with a person who is next to us when they come out of the unconscious mind.

The most prominent feature of infatuation is that a person becomes addicted to a significant other.

Psychologists and philosophers believe that it happens not just because a person loves his or her ideal one, but because he/she loves himself/herself in the company of his/her beloved person. It means we love our images in the minds of other people. This fact proves that a lover has an eye to the main chance from the very beginning. He/she likes himself/herself in his/her new state of mind and tries to keep this wonderful image as long as possible. Infatuation is very often accompanied by pathological jealousy and addiction to a significant other. That is why infatuation is often called an illusion of love. Infatuation is a fool's paradise because the images of each other in the lovers' minds are far from reality.

Sometimes this self-deception lasts for years, which are actually spent in vain. It happens when, because of some reason, it is impossible to get to know the other person better. If you do not know your partner well, it is very easy to create an ideal image. In this regard, living together or just seeing your partner every day often destroys the illusion. It is a very important moment for close relationships. The lovers either realize that everything is nothing more than their whim or they accept each other's weaknesses, truly believing that nobody is free of disadvantages. In this case, infatuation has all the chances to grow into love.

Many thinkers and philosophers in the history have been trying to answer the question what infatuation is. What we know for sure is that infatuation comes and goes rather suddenly.

Infatuation psychology is based on the fact that this feeling turns out to be the biggest factor of a person's development in the future. More often than not it happens when partners accept each other's drawbacks in the end.

Romantic Love

Romantic love is not just a type of love, but a psychological combination of beliefs, ideals, patterns, and expectations. Romantic love does not mean to love; it means to be in love. This is a special psychological phenomenon. Falling in love we believe that we have found the meaning of life, which is in another person. After finding a beloved one we feel integrity. It seems that life is full of super energy that helps us do everything we want, even fly. It looks like a sign of true love. Psychological integrity includes an unconscious requirement for our partner or a spouse to keep up with these deep feelings and joy.

The majority of couples are experiencing high levels of love hormones for two or three years. The woman has enough time to breastfeed the baby, the man has enough time to take care of her. After that the woman is able to survive alone. The romantic period is over. That is why divorces are likely to happen after four years of marriage.

While our minds are full of romance, we are eager to look for romantic love instead of looking for true love. We can have wonderful relationships, but still the lack of intensive romantic emotions often leads to tragic mistakes.

But it is not the point. The myth about romantic love is strongly associated with a romantic ideal of a real man or a real woman. This ideal provides us with a pattern while we are looking for our beloved one. In the end, we are using the pattern to estimate a person we live with. When it turns out that this person is far from being ideal, we feel deeply disappointed.

We are moving heaven and earth to correspond to the ideal of a probable partner. It seems to be a crucial condition of everlasting love. Wonderful, but absolutely unreal. First, these ideals are not ours. They have been imposed on us by our cultural environment. Second, every human being is unique and does not have to correspond to any standards. But we keep confusing somebody else's scenario with real life and unavoidably do not succeed.

Being focused on romantic love we are condemned to fail. First, to be ideal in real life is just impossible. Intensive romantic emotions cannot last long. It is obvious. It means that after the first stage of romantic love is over, we are going to be disappointed and unhappy. Trying to avoid it, we can change partners, looking for a right one. Or we can accept what we have and spend lives with an imperfect person in imperfect relationships.

Second, while we are chasing the shadow of romantic love, our personality is not developing. We do not grow, but keep playing princes and princesses. Since it is just a fairy tale, it makes romantic movies and love stories very popular. Some people believe in them up to a ripe old age.

Third, the most awful thing is that dreaming about romantic love we never find true love, and the life remains fruitless... So, what should we do to escape from such a miserable future? It is simple – we have to start thinking soberly. We should get a romantic pattern out of our minds and to fill them with real thoughts.

Yes, to say is easier than to do. The problem is not only in the cultural trend, which started back in the Middle Ages, but also in the fact that it is very difficult to let a romantic dream go...

We see that the myth about romantic love is very well compatible with a neurotic need for love. The disease will have ascendance over us until we get rid of these neuroses. But practically nothing is impossible. Moreover, the stakes are high – we either live happy and fruitful lives or vegetate dreaming about princes and princesses.

Bonding

Are you still together? It means you are going to bring up a child with this partner. Your body is producing more and more of *oxytocin* – the hormone of tenderness and kindness, as well as *vasopressin* – the hormone of privacy protection and jealousy. It makes you think, "Do not touch what is mine!"

So, romantic love has made way for a calm and soft feeling. After ten years hormonal sources fall into decline because the child has grown up. Love has weakened because its job is done – the next generation is here. But Italian scientists have found that there are people who have initial levels of hormones after 14 years of marriage. Nobody knows for sure why it happens.

At first glance it seems that bonding is all we need to build strong and permanent relationships. In fact, it is a mistake. Bonding is a source of problems for both partners. The dependent one is psychologically tensed all the time. He or she is truly upset when the other partner is not nearby. As a rule, being attached to somebody, we realize this dependency. It provokes the fear of losing a significant other. The significant other does not feel good either. The biggest problem for him or her is too much attention from the other one. Phone calls every hour, "I want to talk to you"... If he or she is going to spend a weekend alone, it will surely hurt the other partner.

Do not be afraid of bonding. It is quite normal. First, ask yourself what attracts you most in your significant other.

A transient bonding is based only on physical feelings, just like infatuation. Women often get hooked on the way a man is dressed, talks, or drives.

If people are in close relationships, bonding appears after some time. Bonding, the habit to be close, and the desire to be close, is a natural ground for love.

Can love be without bonding? Yes, rather often. There are both – love without bonding and bonding without love.

Let us imagine a family. The wife and the husband are constantly arguing, clashing, and feeling jealous. Adrian (the husband) sometimes drinks too much and beats his wife Angelina. But they cannot live without each other, and when Adrian is late from work, Angelina gets really nervous. And if, God save us all, something happens to Angelina, Adrian won't probably survive it. Divorce is unacceptable for both, because they are as one, it would mean cutting in half. "It's so hard to live together, but I'm attached to him too much!" says Angelina. Here we got only bonding, not love.

Imagine another family. You can come to them anytime, they are hospitable, and their home is always cozy. Smiles, joy, and affection... Gordon and Grace are surprisingly attentive to each other and to their children. They arrange for a family party every Saturday and sing altogether! Peace, love, and understanding... But be sure Gordon will stay calm and good even if something happens to Grace or their kids... It is not a mask, it is his soul. He loves his wife and children pretty sincerely, but without bonding. He loves the whole world in the same way.

Of course, here we deal with Great Love, which is full of generous and joyful care.

Love and bonding can be often apart, and it is very easy to confuse them in real life. Besides, we depend on a person we are attached to. Being afraid of losing this person, we have to take care of him or her. We behave almost like lovers. We are attentive to a partner's needs and agree with him or her though it is not what we really want. In this case, bonding resembles love very much. It is a kind of involuntary love. That is why people confuse love and bonding. They speak about love, thinking about bonding, or speak about bonding, dreaming about love.

So, how can we differentiate between the two feelings? There is a very simple criterion, which helps us tell love from bonding. It is pain. Pain when we lose a beloved one. And the fear of it. As a result, we are constantly tensed. Bonding presupposes pain, tension, and dependency. Bonding has more suffering than joy and care. To tell the truth, we often revel in the suffering.

However, bonding is not always bad. Smart people are likely to get attached to those who are going to support them, or who are interesting and useful to them. They prefer not a rigid bonding, but a flexible one. It is like a snap hook used by climbers. When it is necessary, they get attached in a proper way. And they can unsnap the rope anytime.

Bonding is good until you need each other. Until you do not hurt your partner; and it is like a game. But as soon as you feel rigidity and pain in your relationships, be sure danger is close.

You might ask, "Why is it bad to be afraid of losing a significant other?" Living with fear is always a bad thing. Being afraid of loneliness, women agree to relationships with men who are better to stay away from. To make a man stay a woman often turns a blind eye to his disrespect, rudeness, and alcoholism. Fear turns the brain off. It makes a person short-sighted. He or she makes wrong decisions and is unable to think about long-lasting consequences. It is all because of fear...

Women who are not afraid of loneliness are likely to build more reasonable and reliable relationships. Such women can tell their lovers about everything that is important to them calmly and confidently. They put certain limits and do not let men do something unacceptable. Will such a woman love and cherish the beloved one? If her man is a loving husband and a caring father, a reasonable woman will take care of him like of the most expensive jewel. It is really hard to find such a good man. If she is also able to love, she will devote her life to him, thanking her destiny for a wonderful gift. Wise people know that sooner or later everybody goes away. Some people part because of life, others because of death. Those who live in love, but not in bonding are not afraid of death and parting. They remember the beautiful things that they had in the past. And they have an opportunity to do something more beautiful for people who are still with them. It is not indifference, but wisdom. As long as we are alive, those who are nearby need us.

Karmic Love

Karmic love is based on the connection between cause and effect. A soul is immortal. It is sexless and does not remember anything from the previous life. If you did something bad, you will get troubles and suffering in return. It can happen not in this life, but in the next one. If you did something good, you will get a benefit someday, be sure.

Karmic love is not a super prize in a love lottery. It is your unresolved problem from previous incarnations. It's given to clean a bad karma and to correct mistakes of the past. It is better to call it a burdened karma.

Love puts ex-spouses or close relatives together. They greatly offended each other in a past life. They just got trapped and did not manage to find a way out. Now they have an opportunity to fix it. It is unavoidable because it is fate.

Karmic love is always at first sight. A woman sees a man. She is shocked and mentally blocked. Her soul shouts, "It's him!" Passionate love and the flame of feelings fuse the couple together for the period needed to solve a common problem. Sometimes for a few years, but very often the whole life is not enough. Their life is not good, but they cannot break up. Karmic couples are usually childless because children can distract parents from karmic purposes. Suppose a woman got married, gave birth to a child, and became seriously ill. The husband did not support the wife and the child. He cowardly ran away to another woman who was strong and healthy. His wife cursed him; she did not forgive that weak and helpless man. They both burdened their karmas – the first one was irresponsible, the second one was unforgiving. To untie this karmic knot, the couple must correct the mistakes. In the next incarnation they meet in the night club. Love at first sight and quick marriage. After five years, it turns out that the wife is seriously ill. Further events can unfold in different ways:

- The husband works like a horse and supports his family. He cheats on the wife for a change to rest a little. The wife forgives him and is thankful to him anyway. Bingo! The knot is untied. The feelings are slowly dying. It is a typical thing when the purpose of karmic love is achieved. The wife recovers. The husband finds new love. They get divorced. After a while, the ex-wife also gets married. They both feel that they have changed for the better. Their souls are calm, and life is going its way.

- The husband drinks a lot because he cannot bear all these troubles and cheats on his wife. The wife is suffering and crying all the time. They cannot live together, and they cannot break up. In the end, the ill spouse dies. The husband is beating his head against the coffin and feels guilty. In the next incarnation they will meet again. They are doomed to karmic love until they are smart enough to behave in a proper way when in trouble.

Here is the description of karmic relationships given by a woman.

"I still can't explain what attracted me in him. He didn't even match the type of appearance I like. But just after the first conversation I was driven mad. I had no self-control.

He was married, and we didn't see each other very often. I remember this feeling of illness as if I couldn't live without him. We used to say goodbye to each other, and every time I made two steps walking away, my body was aching as if I had flu.

Once he promised to come soon, but didn't show up for several days. He didn't even call me. I woke from stupor on the third day and realized that had eaten almost nothing those days. I'd been sitting by the window all the time.

Only the powers of reason helped me come back to earth. By a tremendous effort of my will I broke up with him. For several months I was shivering when somebody pronounced his name."

The signs of karmic relationships (a woman's view):

- A sudden feeling that he is your man. Love at first sight. You have seen him a couple of times, but you know it is love.

- An uncontrollable physical attraction. Sometimes the body is aching and fevering. Quick and wild sexual contact.

- Lack of self-control. Painful and exhausting emotional stress. You depend on this man.

- You naively trust the person you hardly know. "He's good, he can't fool me".

- Ambitious promises from the very beginning. "I'll save him". "I'll be his wife despite everything". "We were born to be together".

- Heartrending songs, books, and movies get stuck in your head (the Beauty and the Beast, Cinderella, etc). It proves that your relationships are developing according to some scenario.

- It is impossible to leave him even if you understand that you are suffering, and there is no chance to live happily.

These weird feelings arise because the etheric body and the causal body are seriously influencing your physical well-being end emotions.

In other words, it is not love at first sight, but exhausting love from the past. It comes back to make you notice the problem and free yourself and your karmic partner from the burden.

Sometimes it is enough to keep a promise or implement an agreement.

True Love

True love is intended for those who have good karma. This type of love is not always related to our actions in previous incarnations.

True love comes in the two situations.

First: The souls, connected in previous incarnations through good deeds, meet and recognize each other. They could be two female friends, but now one of them is incarnated in a man's body. They could be the brother and the sister, or the aunt and the nephew, it does not matter. In fact, it is a reward for good behavior and right actions in the past life.

Second: love starts between people who are not connected by the previous incarnations, but who are able to get together to a new cycle of development. They are able to get into another society or discover new talents in themselves. Usually love for a new soul is based on consideration and goes from mind to feelings. They both, for example, are working a lot on the same project. Then they decide to get married because they have common interests. The life at work is too lonely and dull. Why not to start a family life?

Such love develops gently and gradually. It does not make you blind or dizzy. At first, it seems rather modest, but it is like a good dinner – the more you eat, the more pleasure you feel. This type of love can last for decades.

Karmic love is not a punishment, but a purpose that needs to be achieved. When the purpose is achieved, karmic love dies. Then it is high time to look for true love. True love is a good thing. And it is not difficult to find it. There are a lot of potential partners around. Every woman can find a man whose soul was very kind to her in previous incarnations. Or she can find the one who is suitable for her now to develop and grow smart together.

Women love men who can help them fulfill themselves. They appreciate men who accept them as they are and push them to become personalities conceived by God or the Cosmos. Not every woman is supposed to be a good angel. She may become a bad fairy, why not? Her only man is connected with her in the energy-information space, according to the plan of Heaven. Sooner or later she will find him. Theoretically, she may never leave her apartment. Some day there will be fire, and a brave fireman will come running to save her. Or a water-pipe will break down, and a handsome plumber will arrive to fix it. It is not quite clear what a woman should do, if the intended man is taken by an accident or an illness. There are two variants – to pass a lifetime alone or wait for the next one. Indeed, there is an intended man for every woman.

A woman always knows when she meets her man. Just after the first meeting she feels surprisingly comfortable and free with him as if they have known each other forever. They have great sex. Living together is not a hard work aimed to start a family, but a natural process, just like breathing. They sometimes quarrel but never torment each other. A woman in love is extremely happy. But all the other aspects of life can go wrong. Remember Bonnie and Clyde who went robbing banks?

Top manager Judy fell in love with a forest ranger Edward and moved to live to his place. She refused from the city comfort and from everything she was used to. But not everybody is ready to rob banks or live in the forest, even for the sake of great love. Therefore, we often give up the intended lover and prefer all other kinds of happiness to happy love.

But what a woman should do if her significant other is supposed to show up after she is fifty? It is reasonable not to wait. Let her have sex and enjoy relationships with other men. When the intended one comes, she will become a character of a wonderful love story. People should never refuse from intended love without trying it. There are not so many things we set heart on. It is up to us to decide which way to go next. But if we lose the chance, it is going to be a big mistake.

A woman usually falls in love with someone who is like her dad. If her dead has never loved her enough, she looks up to a man who used to take care of her when she was a child – her brother, uncle, or grandpa. He becomes a gold standard of a right man to her. She sometimes does not pay attention to men who do not fit the pattern. Men love women who resemble their mothers. It can even be ridiculous. My 30-year-old female friend is complaining that she has been acting more and more like her mother-in-law. The point is that she cannot stand her mother-in-law. But there is nothing to be afraid of. Probably this resemblance is one of the reasons why her husband loves her. She does not get along with her mother-in-law because they are very similar.

The style of a woman's love depends pretty much on the relationships with her father.

The first variant:

Her dad was caring and always loved his daughter. In this case, the woman loves her man not madly. Her feeling is harmonious, with sexual attraction and emotional attachment.

The second variant:

The dad did not love his daughter much or could be far away. He could disappear after the divorce and did not even call her. The woman will be inclined to fall in love at first sight. She hears a velvet voice, and this is it... Such passion is more sexual than emotional. This wild sexual love is justified because it helps break the limits. While the passionate period is going on, she has time to understand who her beloved really is. And she will get attached to him, not always but rather often.

The third variant:

If a girl had no dad, being a woman she is likely to look for bonding. Her ideal is a sugar daddy who is much older than her.

According to this theory, love is always bonding and interdependence. When you lose firm ground, your lover is going to help you. When you feel bad, your partner will come running because you are on the same wavelength. Your health and mood depends on your beloved one. His or her pain is your pain. His or her sadness is your sadness. Nowadays, many people deny bonding and say that being in love one should be independent and free. Run away from such freedom-loving partners. Men of this type are using women all out – sexually, emotionally, and financially – giving nothing back. No regular sex, no empathy, no companionship... Every person has an image of the ideal partner in mind. It includes the appearance and the nature. The image in a woman's mind is called animus, a man's variant is called anima.

Who and Why we Choose

A woman loves a man who has the features of her animus to acquire the necessary part of the man's world. A man loves a woman who fits his anima because he needs his part of the woman's world. In this case, their love is strong and long-lasting. We understand a person quite well if he or she is a part of our personality. That is why there are a lot of unusual couples. For example, a pediatrician who saves the lives of newborn babies, and a scandal column photographer who takes pictures of drunk celebrities and gets paid for that – magazines pay for the pictures, the celebrities pay for non-publication. She loves him because he does not care about limits and morals. He loves her for her kindness and readiness to help children. She also wants to be "a bad girl" who does not think about morals, but she has to hide this desire. It is in her silent man's part. And if the photographer was a woman, he would have been a modest and unselfish one. They love each other not because opposites attract, but because they have many things in common inside.

The Way It Looks

The actions of a person from our world seem logical to us. It is clear that we would have acted in the same way. A woman is likely to forgive her man just like she forgives herself. And he understands that very well. She can let him go on long journeys and wait for his return for years. She lives his life, forgetting about hers. A man who appreciates his woman often takes her back after she was cheating on him (sometimes not once). Sometimes he invests time and money in her career not in his. Such love can last for a lifetime. It does not start right away. Partners need a moment of truth, some push, which helps reveal feelings. This type of love usually starts in trips, at rock festivals, or in an office during a private conversation.

Summing up

There is a striking detail – if a woman never wanted to be a man (just for a while), it is hard for her to love someone. The same applies to men. Such souls have no room for another person. They do not need to admire, understand, and accept him or her.

True love is devoid of selfishness. It does not mean that you have to sacrifice something for someone, forgetting about yourself. You do not have to put your lover's interests over everything else. Without loving yourself, you can never truly love someone. True love, devoid of selfishness, does not mean self-sacrifice. It implies that you do not claim the right to ownership.

This means that loving flowers, you won't pick them to take home and watch them dying slowly. Loving animals, you won't eat meat. Loving nature, you won't make bonfires or break tree branches. Many people often say "I love you" without realizing the meaning of this phrase. They confuse love with the desire to possess. This is as different from love as black is different from white.

True love is not something that comes by itself, falling down on our heads like rain. Love is something that we have to learn. It is not enough to feel fast heart-beating and the desire to fly.

Learn how to love. Learn how to love without claiming the right to ownership.

Imagine snow-covered mountain peaks and their majestic beauty. You like to watch them. You like to breathe fresh mountain air. You get pleasure from the natural splendor that they give you. You love the mountains and watch them without the desire to possess them. You do not want to be the king of these mountains, do you? Are you obsessed with the idea to take these mountains only for yourself? Do you want to prevent other living creatures from admiring them? Of course, you don't. You do not even ask a question if the mountains love you. This is TRUE LOVE. Get it into your life! You should have the same attitude to your husband, wife, and children. Try to love for real. Get selfishness out of your life! Try to love without the desire to dominate. Then you will have nothing to lose or to fear. You will find peace and freedom.

Selfishness and love are incompatible, like light is incompatible with darkness. Selfishness drives love out. It makes love impossible. "I will love you if you love me", "I love you because you are good", "I love you because I feel good with you". These are not true love phrases. True love has no limits. Have you ever noticed how we try to change people sometimes? It is about husbands, wives, children, and friends. We impose our opinions on them. We think we are wiser and more experienced. It is wrong, even if it is from the best of motives. We cannot change anyone if he or she does not want it. A person who knows how to love will never be alone.

Life is going to be kind to the one who knows how to love. Filling the world with true love you will have it back. Any love is true and wonderful in its way when it is in your heart but not in your head.

We recommend you to read a book from our series about **True love: *"Psychology of family relations-the Psychology of love"***